MITZVAH MAGIC

WHAT KIDS CAN DO TO CHANGE THE WORLD

DANNY SIEGEL

WITH NAOMI EISENBERGER

KAR-BEN
PUBLISHING

For Rabbi Neal Gold
Prized Student
Gifted Torah Teacher
Exceptional Friend

I wish to thank the many people featured in this book for allowing me to tell their stories and for supplying me with critical details about their lives and their work.

I also thank the following people for providing additional information and ideas: Jan Nelson, Sandy Levitt, Marc Sternfeld, Sharon Halper, Rabbi Mark Hyman, Arnie Draiman, Miriam Heller, Ilan Glazer, Sam Thrope, Elisheva Gould, Michael Rotjan, Ellen Goldstein, Jeremy Serkin, and Sandy Andron.

My special thanks to Naomi Eisenberger for her help in carefully editing and revising this manuscript. And most of all, to the people at Kar-Ben—Judye Groner and Madeline Wikler—for taking the raw material I sent them, and producing this gorgeous book. —D. S.

To Gerry:
For your patience and your love
To Meital Sarit:
May you learn the lessons of Mitzvah Magic well —N. E.

Library of Congress Cataloging-in-Publication Data

Siegel, Danny.
   Mitzvah Magic: What Kids Can Do To Change the World / by Danny Siegel, with Naomi Eisenberger
      p.   cm.
   ISBN: 1–58013–034–8 (pbk: alk. paper)
   1. Child volunteers—Juvenile literature 2. Social action—Juvenile literature.
   3. Helping behavior—Juvenile literature. 4. Helping behavior—Religious aspects—Judaism. I. Eisenberger, Naomi. II. Title.

Published by Kar-Ben Publishing, Inc., a division of Lerner Publishing Group
241 First Avenue North, Minneapolis, MN 55401
1-800-4KARBEN www.KARBEN.com

Printed in the United States of America
1 2 3 4 5 6 – JR – 07 06 05 04 03 02

CONTENTS

The word *mitzvah* (plural *mitzvot*) technically means commandment, and refers to the entire range of God's commandments that are written in the *Torah*, the first five books of the Bible. These include observing the Sabbath and holidays; keeping the dietary laws (*kashrut*); and providing for sick people, elderly people, and orphans. I use the word *mitzvah* in this book, however, as a synonym for personal acts of goodness, and I have chosen the Yiddish plural, *mitzvahs*, because it traditionally connotes these wonderful deeds.

INTRODUCTION

A revolution is taking place in our nation's religious schools and day schools. Five years ago we would receive an occasional call from a Bar/Bat Mitzvah family who wanted to put more meaning into the simcha. Today these calls are a weekly occurrence, and many of the calls come from kids themselves.

These young people amaze me. If we could track the number of children's books donated, stuffed animals collected, and pounds of food gathered, we would be astounded.

This book tells the stories of dozens of young people (including some *very* young people) who have done incredible things. They are regular people, just like you and me, but they have decided they have the power to do *tikkun olam,* to repair the world.

Each chapter ends with suggestions of projects you and your friends can do, along with names, addresses, phone numbers, and/or websites for these projects. You can also visit our website www.ziv.org for links to many mitzvah websites.

GETTING STARTED

You've heard of the Four Questions asked at the Passover seder. To choose a mitzvah project, ask your-self a new set:

1. What bothers me about the world so much I really *need to change it?*

2. What do I really *like to do?*

3. What am I really *good at doing?*

4. *Who do I know?* You may have special connections with friends or family or a synagogue or school that can make it much easier for you to do mitzvahs.

And a FIFTH QUESTION:

5. *Why not?*

And remember:

• You have awesome mitzvah power in your hands. You don't have to wait until you are 26 or 45 or 61 to make sad people happy, sick people better, or hungry people satisfied with healthy meals. Every age has a unique advantage in the way a person can do mitzvahs. People respond to kids, and especially to "little kids," because they are cute and they exude hope. On their special day, Bar and Bat Mitzvah kids have a captive audience—of family, friends, and congregants. When they speak of mitzvahs, people listen.

• Fixing the world, doing *tikkun olam,* often works better when people join together in their efforts.

• There is no such thing as a small mitzvah. Any mitzvah, no matter how small, changes the entire world.

It feels good to do things for other people, to try to make the world a better place.

To every one of you, I wish you a mighty *yasher koach:* May you have lots of energy to change the world!

—*Danny Siegel*

THE PUSHKA
AND THE BUTTERFLY

I just finished counting the money in my pushka (tzedakah box). It felt a little heavy, but it wasn't full. I found: 69 pennies, 21 nickels, 31 dimes, 43 quarters, and 11 one-dollar bills. Total: $26.59.

I used to think that $26.59 wasn't very much, but that's all changed now, because I know how much Mitzvah Power these coins and bills can have.

Picture a butterfly sitting on a branch of a bush—so many pretty colors, so light, so delicate. All of a sudden, the butterfly takes off and flies away.

Now, the smartest scientists in the world will tell you that the incredibly little bit of wind from the butterfly's wings keeps going on and on and on and can affect the weather all the way in Australia or India. They have a fancy name and difficult math to explain how it works, but it's true.

Some years ago, a 5 1/2 year-old girl named Ellen Goldstein sent me $5 to give away to tzedakah. I thought about how $5 could make a BIG difference, then gave it away to the right place. Is the world a much better place because of 5 1/2 year-old Ellen Goldstein? Of course it is.

WHAT CAN I DO?

1. Count the money in your pushka.

2. Think about what kinds of mitzvahs you can do for $1.27 or $4.45 or $17.91. How many balloons can you buy to give out in a hospital or a shelter? How many boxes of cereal or cans of tuna fish can you buy and donate to a food pantry?

3. If you don't have a pushka, buy or make one.

4. Put pushkas in all the places where you tend to find spare change. Put one in the laundry room for when you empty pockets. Keep one near the living room for coins that fall between the couch pillows. Keep one in your school locker for change you get from vending machines.

Alone

There is a place where we all go
when we must sit alone:
A place where the birds are free to fly,
A place where the sun and its flowers bow in shadow,
A place where the fog is like a veil
and everything is protected,
A place where our souls are set free
and we are allowed to play our own song.

—Samantha Abeel

THE KID WHO GOT IT ALL WRONG IN CLASS

Samantha Abeel began to write her first book of poetry, *Reach for the Moon*, when she was only 13. It was a milestone in her journey of self-discovery.

Samantha has a learning disability. She likes to say, "I learn differently." Her disability is called dyscalculia. She doesn't understand numbers. She can't tell time, has difficulty dialing the right phone number, and if she is buying an ice cream cone, she doesn't know how much change to expect from a $5 bill. Pretty scary, don't you think!

But Samantha does some things very well, among them writing beautiful poetry. In the 7th grade a caring teacher helped her discover her talent and encouraged her to succeed.

Samantha's book of poems also tells the story of her disability and how her mother and teachers helped her deal with her learning problems. "Special education changed my life . . . I could raise my hand in class, even when being taught the most elementary concepts, and say, 'I don't get it,'" she writes.

Through the book, she has taught hundreds of students and teachers about how people learn differently. "L.D. does not mean 'lazy and dumb,' " Samantha explains. "It just means you have another way of looking at the world."

Most important, Samantha has taught children with learning disabilities that it's not their fault that they learn differently. It's how they were made.

And, by the way, even though Samantha can't tell you what time it is, she was graduated from Mt. Holyoke College, Class of 2000—with honors.

WHAT CAN I DO?

1. If you struggle with a disability, listen to what Samantha has to say:

> *The first thing you need to do is find some-thing that you are good at, whether it's singing or skate boarding, an interest in sci-ence or acting, even just being good with people. Then do something with that. If you are good with people, then volunteer at a nursing home or at a day care center; if you love skate boarding, work toward a competi-tion. If it's singing, join a school choir. Even if you can't read music (like me) or read a script, you can always find ways of coping and compensating.*

2. The great sage Hillel said: *What is hateful to you, do not do to others. (Talmud, Shabbat 31a)* Remember never to make fun of someone who can't learn as quickly, or the same way you do. Everyone has things he or she can do really well. We should always look for those things in others. If reading or math comes easy to you, you can help someone who finds it difficult.

CALL TO PROTECT

It is estimated that there are 30 million!! unused cell phones lying around people's houses collecting dust. And the number gets higher every day, as people change carriers or upgrade to fancier phones.

And every one of these unused cell phones has the possibility of actually saving a life.

Organizations that collect cell phones can have them reprogrammed to make free calls to "911," the emergency phone number.

Then they are given free of charge to people who are at risk of abuse, or to the local crossing guard who might have to report an accident, or to an elderly person living alone who might need to get help very quickly. You can probably think of other people who might benefit from a cell phone that is programmed to call 911.

It is an easy way to save lives.

United Hebrew Congregation in St. Louis collected more than 1,000 of them.

Ryan Farber, a young man in Seattle, announced the project in synagogue on Rosh Hashanah, and before Kol Nidre on Yom Kippur synagogue members brought in 150 phones.

At last count, Abby Kerbel of Rockville, MD, had collected more than 230 phones for her Bat Mitzvah Cell Phone Collection Project.

How many do you think you can collect?

WHAT CAN I DO?

1. Start a cell phone project in your school, synagogue, or youth group. It's great to collect the rechargers along with the phones, though the phones alone are still useful. Check out the website www.donateaphone.com for information.

2. Place collection boxes in key places (library, school or synagogue lobby, neighborhood stores).

3. Contact your local police, rescue squad, or domestic violence agency to find out who can reprogram and distribute the phones. Some cell phone stores accept donations.

Only a life lived for others is a life worthwhile.

—Albert Einstein

MITZVAH CENTERPIECES

Noah Fabricant's Bar Mitzvah centerpieces were baskets of brightly-colored woolen scarves, socks, and mittens fashioned to look like flowers. After the event, Noah and his family donated the winter wear to a child welfare organization.

Recyclable Bar/Bat Mitzvah centerpieces are catching on. Tables are decorated with bundles of storybooks, coloring books and crayons, school supplies, board games, and sports equipment which can be donated later to children in shelters, hospitals, and orphanages.

WHAT CAN I DO?

1. Anytime you hear about a luncheon or dinner—a sisterhood book luncheon, teacher recognition, wedding or Bar/Bat Mitzvah, encourage those in charge to consider a recyclable centerpiece.

2. Organize your youth group or class to make and sell reusable centerpieces.

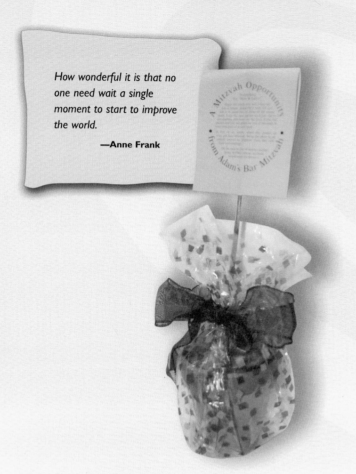

> *How wonderful it is that no one need wait a single moment to start to improve the world.*
>
> **—Anne Frank**

A Mitzvah Opportunity from Adam's Bar Mitzvah

MITZVAH GERANIUMS

I am astonished by how many young people visit elders who live in nursing homes, even people beyond their circle of family and friends. They talk to them and listen to them. They play music or sing with them. Sometimes they lead Shabbat or holiday services or seders.

And some bring plants with them. They give the plants to the residents and tell them, "I brought you a plant as a present. Please take care of it. I'll come back soon to see how you are doing and how the plant is doing."

Why a plant? Some years ago, two researchers, Langer and Rodin,* did a test in nursing homes. They gave some some residents plants and said, "Don't worry about these plants. The aides will take care of them." They gave other residents plants and said to each of them, "This plant is yours to take care of. Please water it, give it sun, and keep an eye on it."

Guess what? They found that the people who had to care for their plants actually lived longer. People need to be needed—to take care of someone or something, even a plant.

What this means is that you may be able to add years to people's lives just by giving them a plant to care for.

Adam Buchoff took this project a step further for his Bar Mitzvah. His family filled clay pots with packets of zinnia seeds and candy. A note inside said, "A mitzvah opportunity. Enjoy the candy now, and when the pot is empty, please use it to plant the seeds. When the zinnias bloom, bring them to an elderly person to brighten his or her day." The back of the note listed assisted-living facilities.

WHAT CAN I DO?

1. Ask the people at a local plant store which plants might be the best for elders to care for.

2. Explain your project to the people at a nursing home or an assisted living facility and get permission.

3. Make an announcement at school and/or your synagogue and get others to join you. Now do it!

* From Ellen J. Langer, *Mindfulness,* Reading, MA: Addison Wesley, 1989.

Shimon the son of
Rabban Gamliel says:
It is not what one says,
but rather what one does
that makes all the difference
in the world.

—Pirke Avot 1:17

THE BIG MUFFIN—I

Victoria Ginsburg teaches 5th grade at Ramaz Jewish Day School in New York. One day, several years ago, when she was on lunch duty, she walked by a trash can and happened to see a big muffin. A perfectly good, un-wrapped, uneaten muffin.

A student decided he didn't want a muffin for lunch that day, so he tossed it in the garbage.

Ms. Ginsburg was shocked. She knew it was wrong to waste food. She knew how many hungry people there are in New York. And she knew that it is a mitzvah to feed people who are hungry.

So she took the muffin out of the trash and brought it to class. At the end of the day she made some phone calls and located an organization called City Harvest. City Harvest picks up good, leftover food from restaurants, hotels, and schools and delivers it to food banks and soup kitchens.

Ms. Ginsberg helped the students organize a food collection. For the last ten years the 4th–6th graders at Ramaz have been in charge of the project. It is called Junior City Harvest.

Each day after lunch, students gather leftover food, from lunches students bring and from the cafeteria—items such as unopened cans of juice, pretzels, or pudding and uneaten fruit. They pack it in bags and boxes and bring it down to a truck that waits outside the school.

Rabbi Elazar says:
*Tzadikkim say little
and do much.*
Talmud—Bava, Metzia, 87a

THE BIG MUFFIN—II
THE SUPER BAR MITZVAH PROJECT

What started as David Levitt's Bar Mitzvah project has changed the way a whole state—Florida—helps feed hungry people.

Because of David's project, more than one million pounds of food have been donated already, and it's growing by more than 225,000 pounds a year.

One day, David noticed that his school cafeteria was throwing out a lot of good food.

He read about a man named Stan Curtis in Kentucky who had gotten restaurants to donate leftover food to shelters and soup kitchens. David called Stan and learned all about what he did.

Then he wrote to Dr. J. Howard Hinesley, the person in charge of the local schools. Dr. Hinesley asked David to prepare a proposal and present it to the entire School Board, which he did—on his 12th birthday.

The board members loved his speech so much, they stood up and clapped for him . . . a kid! Imagine that!

Food for Thought, David's project, was born. David contacted Tampa Bay Harvest, a group of volunteers who picks up leftover food and gives it to soup kitchens and shelters. The rest was details—what kind of containers to use to move the food safely, pick up and delivery times . . . lots of details.

Then the food poured in. Tons and tons of it.

Still, that wasn't enough for David. He decided to try to get schools in the whole state of Florida to participate, and he did it! State law now requires that leftover food be retrieved from public schools, and there is proposed legislation (The David Levitt School Food Anti-Hunger Act of 2001) to further support the idea. The governor even called David to thank him for suggesting the idea.

It will take time to organize the rest of the schools, but it *will* happen. No doubt about it! And it's just waiting to happen in your community as well.

WHAT CAN I DO?

There are lots of food collection programs already in place. Their guidelines can help you set one up at your school or organization.

1. Contact David Levitt's mother, Sandy, at whittle1s@aol.com for materials about Food for Thought.

2. Rock and Wrap It Up!—Syd Mandelbaum's organization (www.rockandwrapitup.org)—organizes food pick-ups from lavish buffets served backstage at rock concerts, from corporate meetings and conventions, and from film, fashion, and commercial events. Contact the director, Aimee Holtzman at aimeezholtzman@aol.com

3. Remember that there is no such thing as a small mitzvah. Do the mitzvah math: If a bagel shop is throwing out 50 bagels a day, that comes to 18,250 bagels a year. Even if you pick up only once a week, you can make a difference.

4. Shelters and soup kitchens are not the only places that can use donated food. For example, one teen-ager brought leftover bagels to the waiting room outside a hospital's intensive care unit, where people wait for news of a friend or relative's condition. The quick snack was just what the anxious people needed for a pick-me-up.

DONATING FOOD TO HUNGRY PEOPLE
A Few Things You Need to Know

The United States Department of Agriculture estimates that we waste nearly 100 billion pounds of food each year. The American government figures that during any month there are at least 12 million households that face hunger.

We can change that.

Before you begin any project that involves donated food, you need to know about the "Bill Emerson Good Samaritan Food Donation Act." This law says that the person who donates food to a non-profit organization that distributes it to hungry people is free of liability.

> *"A person or gleaner shall NOT be subject to civil or criminal liability arising from the nature, age, packaging, or condition of apparently wholesome food or an apparently fit grocery product that the person or gleaner donates in good faith to a non-profit organization for ultimate distribution to needy individuals. (capitalization is author's)*

> *Whatever I want for myself, I want the same for that other person.*
>
> **—Maimonides, Sefer Hamitzvot, Positive Mitzvah #206**

DREAMWEAVERS

PK Belville is not a genie, but she makes dreams come true. Her project, Second Wind Dreams, is one of my very favorite mitzvah projects. PK goes to nursing homes and other places where elders live, asks the residents what their dreams are, and makes them come true. She has helped make 2,000 dreams come true in 400 nursing homes in 38 states, Canada, and India.

Zachary Perry made Second Wind Dreams his Bar Mitzvah project. He learned about Harold Lazeroff who lived in a Jewish nursing home in his community. Mr. Lazeroff, who had not left the nursing home in seven years, wanted to see an exhibit at the art museum, as he had done many times when he was younger. Zachary made it happen. Zachary also met a woman at the home who wanted to see the new baby elephant at the zoo. Done!

Many young people have been involved in making dreams come true. And the wonderful thing is that most of the dreams that people have are so easy to do, and they usually don't cost very much money. More than half of them cost $25 or less.

Dorothy Purrell wanted to see some of her old friends again. When they gathered to be with her, she began to dance.

Mae Bailey, who was blind, wanted to ride all seven of the roller coasters at Six Flags. Her Dreamweaver made it happen.

Sol Lutsky, age 88, didn't have a tallit. His had been destroyed in a fire. So the early childhood students at one of the synagogues bought him a new one.

Wayne Mix, age 81, wanted to swim with the dolphins. Someone else wanted to go fishing. Another wanted a radio with a tape deck, so she could play music for herself. The list goes on and on.

No matter what else you are—a student, a chemist, a store owner, a CEO—when you make a dream come true, you become a Dreamweaver. It's simple. It's fun. It changes lives . . . and it works!

WHAT CAN I DO?

Here's how to start on your road to becoming a Dreamweaver:

1. Visit the Second Wind Dreams website: www. secondwind.org. to learn how it works.

2. Pick a nursing home. Meet with the staff and tell them you want to make some dreams come true.

3. Ask some friends who might also want to become Dreamweavers to join you.

4. Make dreams come true.

> *A person who runs to do just, good, and kind deeds attains life, success, and honor.*
>
> **—Proverbs 21:21**

MERYL AND THE LITTLE MERMAID

Being stuck in a hospital can get scary, and it certainly can get boring. That's why hospitals have a library of videos for kids to watch during the long hours when they have nothing to do.

And that's why Meryl Innerfield decided to collect and donate videotapes to a local children's hospital for her Bat Mitzvah project. She got more than 115 of them, some of them brand new, some of them gently-used. And she is still collecting.

Now that's a fine mitzvah, but Meryl thought about it and decided she could do even better. She arranged for the hospital to let kids take a video home with them, so a young patient who really enjoyed watching *Aladdin* or *Cinderella* could take it home and watch it again and again!

WHAT CAN I DO?

1. There are many, many things in your home and other people's homes that are no longer being used, that others can use: toys, games, books, hats, gloves and scarves, car seats, prom dresses, hearing aids, eye-glasses, sports equipment.

2. There are many organizations that can use your donations. Ask your rabbi, parents, teachers, or local social services professionals for a list.

3. There are some especially good times to mount a collection: Yom Kippur eve when so many people come to synagogue; your birthday; a Bar or Bat Mitzvah; or before Passover, when people are cleaning their houses.

4. Remember that the things you collect should be in good condition. You would not want to receive a jigsaw puzzle with pieces missing!

Tzedakah is not about giving;
Tzedakah is about being.

**—Rabbi Bradley
Shavit Artson**

SWEET MITZVAH MUSIC

By the time he was 15, Michael Rotjan had been play-
ing the violin for a long time. His brother Andrew also
played the violin, his brother Matthew played the cello,
and his mom, Lois, played the viola. And there you had
it, ready to go: a Mitzvah String Quartet. They called
themselves *The Simcha Ensemble.*

Michael was sure there were many people who didn't have a chance to hear nice, live music...such as people in nursing homes and hospitals.

So they organized mitzvah concerts of Jewish tunes and popular melodies, and they played and played and played. The four of them made many people happy using their special talents, and doing what they loved to do.

WHAT CAN I DO?

Pick something you like to do: bake cookies or read books. Say the word "mitzvahs" and see if the two things connect. Many people don't get home-baked cookies and would really like to have some. Others would like to have a book read to them.

We make a living by what we get, but we make a life by what we give.

—**Winston Churchill**

LOCKS OF LOVE

I am losing the hair on the top of my head. It happens to many men. I am not happy about it, but I can wear a hat or an extra large size kippah.

Some people are not so lucky. They lose all of their hair because they have alopecia areata (pronounced a-low-pea-shah air-ee-atah). It can be difficult and embarrassing to lose your hair even for a while, especially for young people.

My friend Peggy Knight started losing her hair when she was 14. Imagine how upsetting it was to be a teenager and feel so different without your hair. Peggy wore hairpieces to feel better, and most people thought it was her own hair.

Her expertise with hairpieces led to her to start Locks of Love.* Kids and adults with long hair volunteer to cut off at least 10 inches of hair and mail it in to the organization. Bunches of hair from many different people are made into attractive hairpieces and given to young people who have lost their own.

When teenagers Ilana Flax and Jessica Zelt heard about Locks of Love, both had their hair cut and donated it. A *Baltimore Jewish Times* story about their mitzvah will hopefully encourage more teens to do the same thing.

WHAT CAN I DO?

1. Go to www.locksoflove.org and learn about the project and how you can donate your own hair.

2. Tell local hair salons about Locks of Love. Ask them to put up a sign encouraging people to donate their hair. Maybe they will even offer free haircuts or discounts to donors.

3. People who have lost their hair can also benefit from used wigs. Donni Engelhart collected used wigs for his Bar Mitzvah project and donated them to Y-ME, a national breast cancer organization.

4. There are other ways to do mitzvahs for those with cancer. Ian O'Gorman, a 5th grader in Oceanside, CA, shaved his hair off before it would fall out from chemotherapy. To soften Ian's embarrassment, many of his classmates did the same, as did their teacher, Jim Alter.

* Peggy is no longer working with Locks of Love, but the organization is still making hairpieces and giving them to young people who need them.

I would say to young people...Let them be sure that every little deed counts, that every word has power, and that we can, everyone, do our share to redeem the world in spite of all the...frustrations and all the disappointments.

—Rabbi Abraham Joshua Heschel

GARDEN of EATIN'

COMMUNITY GARDEN

YOU CAN GARDEN TOO!

A PROGRAM OF
INTERFAITH MINISTRIES
HUNGER COALITION

Sponsored by:
Congregation Beth Yeshurun

THE GARDEN OF EATIN'

Marshall Levit is now 24 and already finished with college. But when I met him, he was just a 14-year-old kid in Houston, who was working on a project to become an Eagle Scout.

Marshall decided that since his synagogue had such a big lawn, you could plant vegetables on a patch of that lawn, and donate them to a food pantry.

The rabbi liked the idea. The president and board of the synagogue did too. And so The Garden of Eatin' was planted at Congregation Beth Yeshurun in Houston.

All kinds of people, young and old, came to work in the garden. Even people who didn't have "green thumbs" could hoe the ground, spread mulch, or pick the peppers and tomatoes. Since 1992, hundreds of pounds of juicy, beautiful vegetables have been given to hungry people.

The garden served other needs as well. Some members of the congregation had moved from their houses when their children were grown. They no longer had a place to garden until Marshall Levit came along.

Rachel Margolin was 9 years old when she convinced her synagogue in Southfield, Michigan, to plant a Mitzvah Garden. In its very first summer it was bursting with luscious vegetables just waiting to be harvested and donated to hungry people.

WHAT CAN I DO?

1. Walk all around your synagogue property and see if there is a place for a Mitzvah Garden. Ask your rabbi or synagogue president for permission to present your idea to the board.

2. Get the names of people in the congregation with a talent for growing vegetables. If your synagogue is not a good place, try the Jewish Community Center, a nursing home, or a school.

3. Plant flowers, too, so you can pick them and bring them to nursing homes and hospitals.

THE MOST BEAUTIFUL
SONGS IN THE WORLD

My friend John Beltzer says he is only 6'4", but I think
he is a lot taller than that. Whenever I see him and give
him a hug it feels like he is at least 7'8". He's a giant,
a Mitzvah Giant.

He makes people happy with his songs. He and his friends write, sing, play, and record special songs for kids who are very, very sick. Each song is written for and about that one child, and it's called "Mark's Song" or "Debbie's Song." The child gets the recording in the mail or sometimes personally delivered by the song-writer or singer.

You can imagine how it must feel to be in and out of the doctor's office or hospital getting scary and painful treatments. But for many kids it isn't so hard any more, because they all have songs of their own which they can play or sing over and over again. Some doctors have told John that painful tests aren't that painful any more when the child is listening to his or her song.

John and his friends have written over 2,700 of these songs. Today they are writing about 70 new ones each month. John uses his talent and caring to make kids happy.

Demi Lada

D. Obadia

WHAT CAN I DO?

1. Visit John's website: www.songsoflove.org and learn all about his mitzvah songs.

2. If you know a sick child, have a family member, doctor, or social worker fill out a Songs of Love® application form. It asks the child's name and nickname, and information about his or her interests, pets, favorite books or movies, anything that will help the writers make the song special.

3. Let hospitals, doctors, nurses, and social workers know about Songs of Love. Encourage them to get the forms and to have family members fill them out, so John and his people can write a song.

4. Encourage the cantor in your synagogue, or your school choir or any group of people who enjoy singing to perform one of the songs.

THE GREAT STUFFED ANIMAL MITZVAH

Aviva Kieffer just knew that there were many kids who didn't own even one teddy bear.

For her Bat Mitzvah, she asked people to bring her as many stuffed animals as they could, to donate to children in shelters, hospitals, and institutions. Bears, lions, elephants, came pouring in...a few hundred of them! People really wanted to be a part of her Mitzvah.

A similar program was begun by Merrily Ansell, a grown-up! After her sister died following a long battle with cancer, Merrily vowed that she would do something to help people undergoing stressful chemotherapy.

Books, Bears and Bonnets® is her response. Patients entering treatment in any one of ten hospitals in the Washington, DC area are given a colorful box containing a cuddly teddy bear, a snappy cap, and a book.

Merrily has distributed more than 750 boxes in less than a year.

WHAT CAN I DO?

1. Sometimes the hard part is trying to figure out where to donate the things you collect. Start by asking at your local police department or rescue squad. Officers like to keep stuffed animals in their trunk to give to children they meet in the course of investigating an accident or fire.

2. Then ask at social service agencies or shelters. It won't be hard to find the right place. Who doesn't need a stuffed animal to cuddle once in a while?

3. Contact Merrily at manmd@starpower.net to find out more about Books, Bears, and Bonnets. This is a great project for a Bar or Bat Mitzvah.

Whoever saves a single life
it is as if that person had
saved an entire world.

—Mishna Sanhedrin,
Chapter 4

COMPUTER MITZVAHS

In July of 1995, my friend Jay Feinberg, who was suffering from leukemia, had a bone marrow transplant. He now lives with the bone marrow of a woman named Becky, who got tested especially for him. But it took four years until Jay found a suitable donor. None of his family—even distant aunts and uncles and cousins—matched.

So members of the Feinberg family rolled up their sleeves and organized bone marrow drives everywhere. They went from coast to coast, and even to distant countries to try find a match.

Because he found *his* match, Jay decided to look for matches for others. He started The Gift of Life Bone Marrow Foundation, Inc. which organizes drives to get people tested, and serves as a resource for people who need transplants.

Jay couldn't do his work without his computers. He uses them to manage enormous amounts of data. Jay has saved more than 400 lives by matching donors to people who need the transplants.

WHAT CAN I DO?

1. Go to www.bone-marrow.org—the Gift of Life website—and learn as much as you can about bone marrow and stem cell transplants.

2. Encourage your synagogue to organize a bone marrow drive. Every new person who is tested may save a life. (I have three friends who have donated their bone marrow and saved other people's lives.)

3. Think of all the ways you can use your computer for mitzvahs. One of the best things you can do is teach elders to use a computer. They can use it to surf the web, to e-mail family and friends, to write personal histories, fiction and poetry, and to prepare a family tree.

4. You can use computers for other mitzvahs as well—to make signs such as "Bring in cans of food next Sunday," or "Recycle your unused cell phone." You can design birthday cards and holiday cards to send to people who live all alone.

5. If you are a hardware expert, you can upgrade old computers and donate them to others who don't have them. Most kids are better than adults at this!

It's not what you are,
but what you don't
become that hurts.

—**Oscar Levant**

ELVIS THE MAGICAL
MITZVAH HORSE

Elvis the Mitzvah horse doesn't race in races, and he doesn't pull wagons full of hay or peaches. He does mitzvahs. And he's only ten years old!

He is a beautiful, gentle and very patient horse, and his owner, Anita Shkedi, is a very special person. She is an expert in therapeutic horseback riding—using horses to make people better. Anita and her husband Giora run INTRA, the Israel National Therapeutic Riding Association.

Therapeutic horseback riding can help people with physical disabilities such as cerebral palsy, multiple sclerosis, and head injuries, as well as learning and emotional disabilities.

There are many reasons why. A horse's steady pace exercises the rider's body and helps the functioning of the heart and circulatory system. Riding helps develop a person's communication and memory skills. The opportunity to sit high on a horse increases self-esteem. And riders develop a warm, caring relationship with their new friend, the horse.

About a year ago a teen-ager came up to me and said, "Danny, after I heard you talk about Anita last summer, I told my aunt who has MS. She's been riding, and she isn't using a wheelchair any more, at least for now." Wow!

WHAT CAN I DO?

1. Not many people know about therapeutic horseback riding. You can make a big difference just by telling others about its benefits. Contact the North American Riding for the Handicapped Association to learn about their 700 riding clubs. (www.NARHA.org)

2. Visit your nearest club and learn from the therapists. Post information on bulletin boards in your synagogue and school. Tell your doctor, your rabbi, your teachers. Some day soon, you may be able to say to yourself, "Someone who used to use a wheelchair has left it behind—at least for a few months—and is walking, just because I did a little bit of mitzvah work."

The Good People everywhere will teach anyone who wants to know how to fix all things breaking and broken in this world—including hearts and dreams—and along the way we will learn such things as why we are here and what we are supposed to be doing with our hands and minds and souls and our time.

—Danny Siegel, Heroes and Miracle Workers

THE MITZVAH MAGICIAN

Everyone knows who David Copperfield is. He's the most famous magician in the world. He's also the most famous illusionist, which means he can make you think you see things that really aren't there.

He levitated a Ferrari. (At least that's what people thought.)

He walked through The Great Wall of China. (Or so it seemed.)

He can do card tricks and pull rabbits out of hats, but those are really too simple for him.

His real name is David Kotkin, and once upon a time he was a little Jewish kid from New Jersey who liked to do magic tricks. Then he became famous and rich. What most people don't know is that he is also a great Mitzvah Man. He invented Project Magic. It's all about how hands work.

As you know, some people's hands don't work as well as "normal" hands. Because of an accident or illness, they may not be able to do things such as button buttons or tie shoelaces. Physical and occupational therapists (PTs and OTs) work with these people to increase their dexterity. And now, because of David Copperfield, "magically" they are being more successful.

In more than 30 countries and 1100 hospitals around the world, PTs and OTs are learning sleight-of-hand magic tricks and teaching them to their patients. As Copperfield explains, "It motivates a patient's therapy and helps to build self esteem."

Now here is the most important part of the story: David Copperfield, who can make his audiences see things that aren't really there, says, "There is nothing I do that is more important (than Project Magic)."

WHAT CAN I DO?

1. To learn more, log onto Project Magic's website www.allstarcharity.com/davidcopperfield.html

2. Go to a local hospital and ask if the physical and occupational therapists know about Project Magic. If they haven't heard about it, give them a print-out from the website so they can learn how to do this special kind of magic.

> *Never doubt that a small group of thoughtful, committed citizens can change the world; indeed, it's the only thing that ever does.*
>
> **—Margaret Mead**

MITZVAH INVENTIONS

How often do you have to wait until after 4 p.m. to meet a mitzvah hero because she first has to come home from elementary school? That's what I had to do when I went to meet Kimberly Cook, who at age nine invented a beeper with Braille numbers on it, so blind people could get their messages whenever it was convenient for them . . . and have the same privacy as sighted people. It was Kimberly's school science project.

WHAT CAN I DO?

Others have thought of mitzvah ideas and projects that no one else ever thought of. Maybe you can, too!

1. Someone thought to put puffy, balloon-type tires on wheelchairs, so that people who use them can go right up to the edge of the water onto the beach—and even into the water.

2. One synagogue thought to give out balloons on Rosh Hashanah and at the end of Yom Kippur to members of the congregation who are deaf. Why balloons? Because deaf people can feel the vibrations of the sounds of the shofar by holding the sides of the balloons.

3. Someone thought it would be a good idea to put tennis balls with a hole in them on the bottom of the legs of a walker, so that people using them wouldn't slip or skid.

4. Some also thought to put tennis balls on furniture legs to eliminate ambient noise in classrooms where children are wearing hearing aids.

If you and your friends sit down and think real hard, you might also "invent" fabulous mitzvah projects.

Nobody makes a greater mistake than he who does nothing because he could only do a little.

—Edmund Burke

THE GOURMET DOGGIE NOSH MITZVAH

Yoav Nessim's Bar Mitzvah mitzvah project centered on—of all things—doggy treats. You know, the nosh you give your boxer or lab just for being a good friend.

Yoav never owned a dog, but he loves dogs and he loves mitzvahs. So Yoav and his family got a recipe for fancy gourmet dog goodies and baked up a batch. They looked like little brownies. Yoav and his family sold them for $5 a bag, hoping to raise $500 for the Israel Guide Dog Center for the Blind. By the time the project was over, Yoav did a lot better than that. He raised $1,760!

The good new is that dogs loved the goodies. And the really good news is that more blind people in Israel have a better chance of getting a guide dog because of Yoav's project.

GOURMET DOGGIE BISCUITS

1 1/4 lb. chicken livers   *milk or water as necessary*
4 c. self-rising flour   *chopped dill or thinly*
4 eggs   *grated carrots (optional)*

Mince chicken livers. Add flour and eggs. Add dill or carrots for variety. Mix thoroughly and add liquid until the mixture is the consistency of cake batter.

Pour the mixture into lightly oiled baking pans. You should have enough for 3 pans (8" x 8").

Bake for 45 minutes at 350°. Cut into one inch squares. Return to the oven for another 45 minutes. Turn the biscuits over, lower the oven temperature to 250° and put back into the oven for an hour. Turn off the oven and let biscuits cool there overnight until completely dry.

WHAT CAN I DO?

1. Visit the Israel Guide Dog's website at: www.israelguidedog.org to learn about this fantastic group of people who have matched more than 150 people and guide dogs in Israel since it started in 1991.

2. See if your community has a guide dog center and find out how you can support their work. Maybe your family can even offer to raise a puppy.

3. Think of other things you can bake to raise money. Maybe a high-class mitzvah bird nosh!

Rabbi Simla'i explained in a sermon: The Torah begins and ends with acts of caring and lovingkindness.

—Talmud, Sota

STARTED BY KIDS...
RUN BY KIDS

Not all children have a happy home life, and when their parents cannot care for them, some have to move to other people's homes. They become "foster children". When that happens, they have to pack up everything they own and carry their belongings to their new home.

Makenzie Snyder, who lives in Washington, DC, was 7 years old when she heard that many foster children don't have suitcases. They are forced to move their belongings in plastic garbage bags. That made her angry. Who wants to put favorite things—toys or dolls or clothes—into a garbage bag?

So she started to collect duffel bags and suitcases for these foster children. Makenzie puts a stuffed animal and a personal note into each one. The note says, "God told me you could use a duffel bag and a cuddly friend. So, I send this with love to you."

Sometimes a little mitzvah can turn into a HUGE mitzvah. Makenzie's story was written up in *The Washington Post.* Shortly after, she got a call from the White House inviting her and her family to attend a news conference. She spent time chatting with President Clinton who promised to donate duffel bags himself.

Then *People* magazine arrived to do a photo shoot. And Makenzie's project was even featured in an issue of the Lands' End catalog. The company donated bags and bears and is asking their customers to do the same.

WHAT CAN I DO?

1. Go to www.childrentochildren.org, Makenzie's website, and read all about this amazing young person.

2. Go to www.suitcasesforkids.org, the website for Aubyn Burnside. She started a project just like this—in 1995 in Hickory, NC—when she was 10 years old. It has spread to every state in the U.S. and many other countries. Aubyn's site has a "starter kit" to help you develop a program in your commuity.

3. Check with Foster Care and Child Welfare agencies in your community to see if they have a program or would like you to start one.

4. Think about other kids who can use suitcases or bookbags, such as kids who go to camp on scholarship, or kids whose families can't afford to buy them school bags.

*Whatever you can do,
or dream you can do,
you can.*

—Goethe

AVSHALOM, ANTOINE, AND DOOBIE

In life, things can get damaged or broken, including people's bodies and sometimes their minds.

There are many ways to fix things when a body or mind is hurt. Sometimes exercise helps, or changing the way you eat. Other times medicines or surgery or therapy can fix things.

Enter: Avshalom, a human being who lives in Israel.

Enter: Doobie, a "kena'an," a beautiful dog, with only three legs.

Enter: Antoine, a ragdoll cat.

Avshalom does mitzvahs which involve saving injured and abused animals. But I think his greatest mitzvah is Animal Assisted Therapy or AAT.

Avshalom knows that sometimes people who are hurt or sad, or terribly lonely can get better if there is a friendly cat or dog to help out. If you own a dog or a cat, you probably already have this figured out. You talk to the animal or pet it or play with it, and you feel better.

Antoine and Doobie are two of the animals Avshalom works with to help people.

Some people with disabilities look at Doobie and they say, "He seems very happy, even though he is missing a leg. I think I can be happy, too."

Avshalom calls his Mitzvah project HAMA IL, which is short for Humans and Animals in Mutual Assistance in Israel. A perfect name. Humans help animals; animals help humans.

WHAT CAN I DO?

1. E-mail Avshalom (avshalom_beni@hotmail.com.) and tell him what wonderful work he is doing.

2. Go to Delta Society's website: www.deltasociety. org to learn more about AAT and PAT (pet-assisted therapy)

3. Ask your veterinarian to give a talk about AAT/PAT at your school, synagogue, or youth group.

4. E-mail Vicky MacKay at vmackay9@aol.com and ask her about the good AAT/PAT work she does with mitzvah dogs and mitzvah birds.

5. Think of ways you can get animals and humans to work with each other to make life better. For example: A man named Ira Morris had a truck stop in Arizona. He knew how lonely it could be for truckers out on the road, so he had a cat and a rocking chair waiting for the drivers when they would stop for gas. Just to give them a few minutes of companionship. Not a bad idea. Good mitzvah thinking.

GLOSSARY

Bar/Bat Mitzvah: The coming-of-age for a Jewish child. Boys become Bar Mitzvah (literally "adult mitzvah person") at 13; girls become Bat Mitzvah at 12 or 13. The occasion is marked with a synagogue service. The child often leads the prayers, is called to the Torah, and addresses the congregation. A party usually follows!

Kippah: Yarmulke, skullcap

Kol Nidre: The evening service before Yom Kippur

Mensch: A good and decent human being

Pushka: A tzedakah box used to collect charitable contributions

Rosh Hashanah: Jewish New Year

Seder: The ritual meal that ushers in Passover at which time the story of the Exodus from Egypt is read

Shabbat: The Jewish Sabbath

Shofar: Ram's horn blown on Rosh Hashanah and Yom Kippur

Simcha: Celebration

Tallit: Prayer shawl

Tikkun Olam: Repairing the world

Tzedakah: Literally "justice." Refers to money collected for charitable causes

Yom Kippur: Day of Atonement, the holiest day of the Jewish Year

CREDITS

Cover photos courtesy Avshalom Beni, Merrily Husell, Madeline Wikler and Rotjan family.

ABOUT THE AUTHORS

Danny Siegel, author, lecturer, and poet, is known for his tzedakah teaching and work with Ziv Tzedakah Fund, which has distributed over $5 million to social service projects world-wide. He was one of three recipients of the 1993 Covenant Award for Exceptional Jewish Educators. His books for teens and adults include *1+1=3 and 37 Other Mitzvah Principles to Live By; Heroes and Miracle Workers; Healing: Readings and Meditations; Tell Me A Mitzvah;* and the poetry anthology, *A Hearing Heart.*

Naomi Eisenberger is the Managing Director of Ziv Tzedakah Fund and the project manager of the Ziv Giraffe Curriculum. A former high school social science teacher, she frequently speaks to school and adult audiences about Ziv and its mitzvah heroes.